HOW Kids LIVED

A KID'S LIFE IN
ANCIENT EGYPT

SARAH MACHAJEWSKI

PowerKiDS
press.

New York

Published in 2015 by The Rosen Publishing Group, Inc.
29 East 21st Street, New York, NY 10010

First Edition

Editor: Sarah Machajewski
Book Design: Michael J. Flynn

Photo Credits: Cover (Egyptian painting) DEA/G. LOVERA/De Agostini/Getty Images; cover, pp. 1, 3, 4, 6, 8, 10, 12–16, 18, 20, 22–24 (background texture) Ozerina Anna/Shutterstock.com; pp. 3, 4, 6, 8, 10, 12–16, 18, 20, 22–24 (paper) Paladin12/Shutterstock.com; p. 5 sculpies/Shutterstock.com; p. 6 llepet/Shutterstock.com; p. 7 Rogers Fund, 1930/The Metropolitan Museum of Art; p. 9 WitR/Shutterstock.com; p. 11 ostill/Shutterstock.com; p. 13 De Agostini/G. Dagli Orti/Getty Images; pp. 14, 21 Leemage/ Universal Images Group/Getty Images; p. 15 Patryk Kosmider/Shutterstock.com; p. 17 Kenneth Garrett/National Geographic/Getty Images; p. 19 DEA/G. DAGLI ORTI/Getty Images; p. 22 Matej Kastelic/Shutterstock.com.

Library of Congress Cataloging-in-Publication Data

Machajewski, Sarah.
A kid's life in ancient Egypt / by Sarah Machajewski.
p. cm. — (How kids lived)
Includes index.
ISBN 978-1-4994-0021-2 (pbk.)
ISBN 978-1-4994-0015-1 (6-pack)
ISBN 978-1-4994-0014-4 (library binding)
1. Egypt — Social life and customs — To 332 B.C. — Juvenile literature. 2. Children — Egypt — Juvenile literature. 3. Egypt — Civilization — Juvenile literature. I. Machajewski, Sarah. II. Title.
DT61.M34 2015
305.23—d23

Manufactured in the United States of America

CPSIA Compliance Information: Batch #CW15PK: For Further Information contact Rosen Publishing, New York, New York at 1-800-237-9932

CONTENTS

ONE OF THE FIRST CIVILIZATIONS

Ancient Egypt was one of the world's first civilizations. It began over 5,000 years ago in North Africa. Between 3100 BC and 30 BC, ancient Egyptians built a society that gave the world important objects that are still around today, such as pyramids, temples, paper (made from papyrus plants), locks and keys, and more.

Most people think of pharaohs, or kings, and queens when they think of ancient Egypt, but there was more to the society than its most important rulers. The common people of Egypt led interesting lives, too. Let's learn about ancient Egypt through the life of a boy named Shen.

Remains of ancient Egypt, such as these pyramids, have lasted for thousands of years.

THE MIGHTY NILE RIVER

Shen lived during the **reign** of Ramesses II, one of ancient Egypt's greatest rulers. Ramesses II built cities, temples, and monuments throughout the land he ruled. The cities were busy and full of people, but the most important part of this civilization was something natural—the Nile River.

Ancient Egypt developed along the Nile River because it provided water and rich soil for farming. The Nile also acted as a kind of water highway. Egyptians used the river to carry the goods they traded with other civilizations. Egyptians like Shen's family couldn't have survived without the Nile River.

The Nile flooded every spring. The floods left behind rich, black soil that farmers used to grow healthy crops.

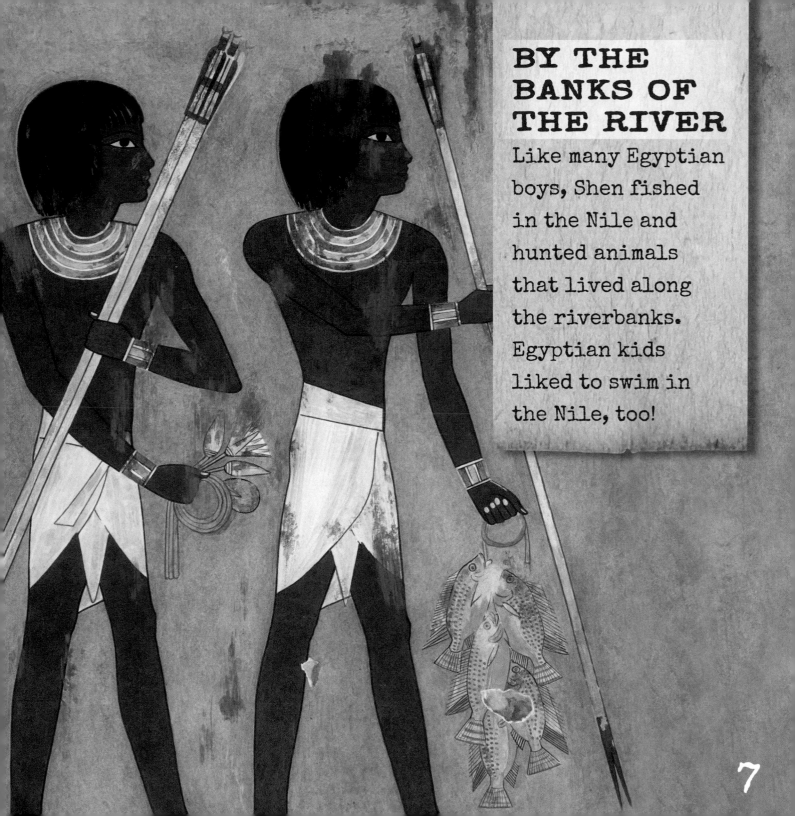

BY THE BANKS OF THE RIVER

Like many Egyptian boys, Shen fished in the Nile and hunted animals that lived along the riverbanks. Egyptian kids liked to swim in the Nile, too!

LIFE IN MEMPHIS

Shen and his family lived in Memphis, a city near the northern end of the Nile. Memphis had many palaces and temples. The biggest was the Hout-ka-Ptah—a temple that honored Ptah, the god of builders and craftsmen.

Many Egyptians in Memphis were craftspeople. They made and sold cloth, tools, bricks, and **jewelry**. Shen loved to visit the shops in town and see the goods sold there. Memphis also had many farmers, including Shen's father. His family lived at the edge of the city, where there was enough land to grow crops and raise animals.

Shen would've seen statues such as the sphinx shown here all over Memphis.

9

HOME SWEET HOME

Ancient Egyptians used **resources** in their surroundings to build their homes. Egyptians made bricks out of mud. They dried them in the sun, then used the bricks to build houses. Shen's house had small windows to keep out the sun and keep the house cool. The roof was flat. On very hot nights, Shen was allowed to sleep on the roof!

The floor in Shen's house was made of dirt. His mom used leaves from palm trees to make mats that covered the floor. Shen's house had a **courtyard** where they kept their oven and stored food.

Egypt's weather is very hot. Egyptian homes were built to keep people cool and keep out as much heat as possible.

UNDER ONE ROOF

Everyone in Shen's family slept in the same room, since their house only had one room to share!

CLIFF HOMES ALONG THE NILE

11

HARD AT WORK

There was a lot of work to do on the farm. Shen's dad used their oxen to pull a plow, which is a tool that turns over soil. Plowing made the soil good for growing crops.

Shen helped his dad plant seeds, but his favorite job was picking fruits and vegetables when they were ripe. Shen and his dad often visited other farmers to trade food. This allowed them to enjoy different kinds of foods without having to grow it all themselves. Egyptian women helped on family farms, too. Shen's mom ran the farm when his dad got sick.

This image shows an Egyptian man holding a whip, which he uses to make the oxen pull the plow.

A HELPING HAND

Egyptian parents needed their kids to help with all the work on the farm. Sons often took over the farm when their parents were too old or too sick to work.

DINNERTIME

Ancient Egypt didn't have grocery stores like we have today. Instead, Egyptians had to grow and raise their own food. Shen's family grew grains, onions, beans, dates, and figs. They raised goats and sheep. They also fished in the Nile and hunted animals such as duck and geese for meat.

Egyptian women were in charge of cooking for their family. Shen's mom cooked all their food in a clay oven. She also ground grain into flour to make bread. Her bread was Shen's favorite food!

This statue shows an Egyptian woman making bread.

SOMETHING SWEET

Shen's favorite dessert was fruit, such as figs.

Most Egyptians, including Shen's family, used an oven made of clay to cook their food.

15

KEEPING COOL

Ancient Egyptians wore clothes that kept them cool in Egypt's hot weather. Most clothes were made of linen, which is a light and airy cloth. Men wore **kilts**. Shen wore a kilt like his dad, but he wrapped it between his legs and around his waist. Shen's mom wore long linen dresses.

Another way Shen kept cool was by shaving his head. Like many boys at the time, Shen shaved off all his hair except for one lock on the side of his head. Women and girls wore their hair in braids. Both men and women wore jewelry and makeup.

FULLY CLOTHED

Kids in ancient Egypt didn't have to start wearing clothes until they were about six years old. Then, they wore clothes that looked like their parents' clothes.

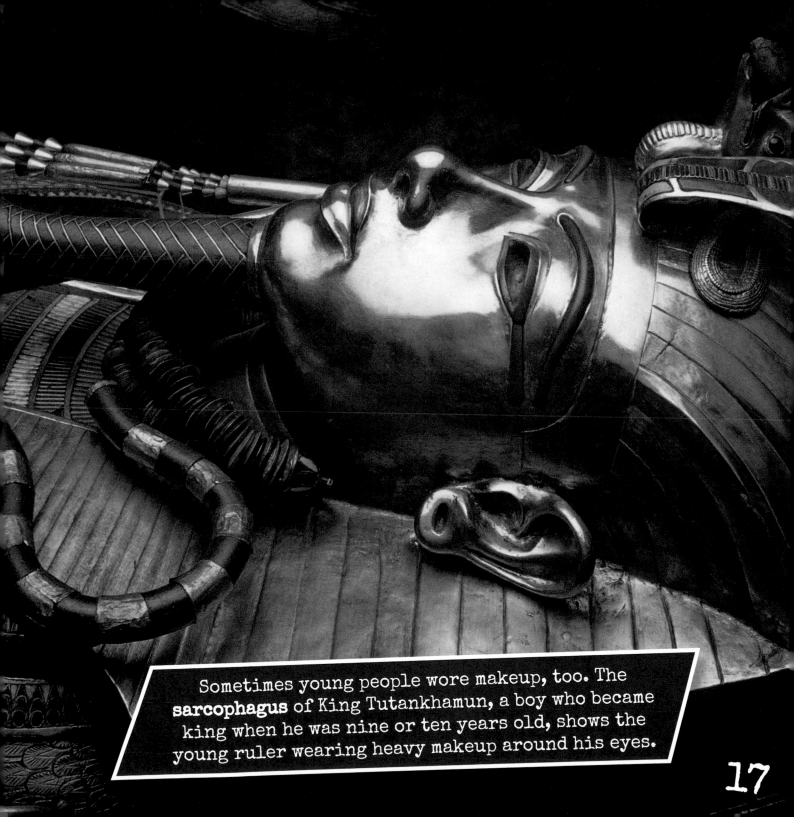

Sometimes young people wore makeup, too. The **sarcophagus** of King Tutankhamun, a boy who became king when he was nine or ten years old, shows the young ruler wearing heavy makeup around his eyes.

READING AND WRITING

Not all ancient Egyptians knew how to read and write. That's because only some Egyptians went to school. They were often boys from rich families. Boys from poor families, such as Shen's, and girls didn't go to school.

Egyptians who knew how to read and write were called scribes. They read hieroglyphics (hy-ruh-GLIH-fihks), which is a kind of writing that uses pictures to stand for words or ideas. Scribes often became **priests**, tax collectors, or doctors, or took jobs recording spells and important **religious** texts. We've learned much about ancient Egypt from studying scribes' writing.

Boys whose fathers were scribes often became scribes themselves. They took on their father's job once they completed their education.

19

THE AFTERLIFE

Religion was a big part of life in ancient Egypt. People believed gods and goddesses controlled all parts of their life, such as how crops grew, what the weather was like, and when good and bad things happened. Egyptians built temples to honor their gods and made offerings to keep them happy.

Ancient Egyptians believed in life after death. Pharaohs and queens had pyramids built and filled them with objects they needed in the **afterlife**. The most important object needed in the afterlife was a person's body, so pyramids also contained mummies.

Wealthy Egyptians paid to have their bodies **preserved** through a process called mummification. Poor people preserved their bodies by burying them in sand. The hot, dry sand mummified bodies naturally.

TEMPLE OFFERINGS

Shen and his family visited the temples in Memphis to make offerings to their gods. They hoped their offerings would bring a good **harvest** and good fortune to their family.

REMAINS OF THE PAST

Shen's life in ancient Egypt was busy with work, but he still found time for fun. He and his friends played with spinning tops and balls. They also played a board game called senet. Shen was very good at this game!

Shen was just one ancient Egyptian who lived during a time of great discoveries and advancements. This **culture** gave us libraries, a special kind of paper, and the 365-day calendar we still use today. Ancient Egyptian society ended more than 2,000 years ago, but we can learn about its people by studying the great writings and remains they left behind.

GLOSSARY

afterlife: Life after death.

courtyard: A small outdoor space in the center of a house.

culture: The beliefs and ways of life of a group of people.

harvest: The crops that are picked during a growing season.

jewelry: Pieces of metal, plastic, or other matter worn as decoration.

kilt: A knee-length skirt.

preserve: To keep something in its original state.

priest: A person who performs religious ceremonies.

reign: The period of time during which a king or queen rules.

religious: Relating to or believing in a religion.

resource: Something in nature that can be used by people.

sarcophagus: A stone coffin displayed aboveground.

INDEX

WEBSITES

Due to the changing nature of Internet links, PowerKids Press has developed an online list of websites related to the subject of this book. This site is updated regularly. Please use this link to access the list: www.powerkidslinks.com/hkl/egyp